Reflections

and

Resurgence

Daniel Wiita Livingston

Table of Contents

Acknowledgements

To all those who have gone before me and to everyone who supported me along the way, I know it wasn't easy.

All I can say is, thank you!

William Livingstone Memorial Lighthouse
Detroit, Michigan
Photo by Daniel Wiita Livingston

One the Fresh-Water Shores, My Palace Stands Alone

I walk underneath the children who have climbed the trees,
The trees that reside on the lawn of my palace, my labor, my sanctuary.

This is my castle.
Always has been,
As I plan to die.

As I planned to die here?
Will I die here?
Before, I was so sure,
And now I am not.

I can go anywhere.
Always have, always will.

Destiny planned.
Destination set.
Directions picked.
Departure had.
Determination steadfast.

Weeks later,
This letter...

From the depths of a personal odyssey, one that has unfolded beneath
the boughs of the ancient trees this evening on the adorning lawns of
my estate. This sanctuary, my labor's fruit, stands as a testament to a
city's work, a castle of artistic dreams where I once believed my final
chapter could be penned.

Yet, as I traverse this familiar landscape, a new realization dawns upon
me. The certainty of destiny's plan, once as steadfast as the towering
oaks, now wavers like leaves in the wind. The paths I've walked with
such determination now branch into unforeseen directions, and the
letter I hold in my hand is a harbinger of change, a missive from the
depths, as if Poseidon himself has cast a net of illusion and mastery
over my realm.

In this maelstrom of emotion, where madness once breached the gates
only to be repelled, it now dances with a chaotic grace, inviting me to
embrace the tumultuous sea of change. It is a different kind of madness,

9

one that oscillates between resistance and ecstasy, fear and enlightenment.

For in the heart of chaos, there lies a luminous truth, and it is in this truth that new horizons may yet be discovered.

On my journey of becoming hyper-aware and the intricate dance between discipline and creativity that has defined my path, and carved a unique paradox.

For years, I have sought the wisdom of an Apollonian mind, tempered with the discipline of a semi-stern Christian ethos. Yet, the Dionysian call to embrace the wild and untamed aspects of my nature has been equally compelling. In a world that often prioritizes efficiency over artistry, I have witnessed the systematic dismantling of creative sanctuaries, replaced by the stark pragmatism of glass and concrete. In 2016, the plans were set out to dismantle a world I had built since a child. One by one, piece by piece, it was unceremoniously taken down with no regard to its history. In silence, it was pulled apart. What took decades to erect took two years to have it torn down, and by 2018, what was left was bulldozed by the hands of another.

Despite the relentless march of modernity, the Dionysian flame within me remained unextinguished despite the dousing of water I tried to hose it with from my firefighting disciplines, and for other external influences. A testament to the futility of trying to suppress the primal essence of our being. This internal conflict, akin to a meticulous surgery, has left its mark, carving out the madness while preserving the core of its purpose.

In my quest for survival, I have cultivated a hyper-awareness of my emotions and physical being, attuning to their nuances with a precision that eludes most. Granting me insight while often rendering me silent in the face of others' astonishment at the depths of what lies beneath.

The complexities of our existence, I believe it is crucial to honor both the disciplined and the untamed within us. It is in this balance that we find the truest expression of our humanity. A suppressed flame can indeed conflagrate rapidly when reintroduced to an oxygen-rich atmosphere. This phenomenon aligns with the behavior of fire in oxygen-enriched environments, where flammable materials, even those not typically considered a risk, can ignite more easily and burn more vigorously.

Furthermore, a fire that appears to be extinguished may still pose a significant threat. A "wild flame" that has not been completely extinguished can reignite under the right conditions, particularly when oxygen levels are increased, leading to a rapid escalation of fire intensity. Every time I have a reminder of you, oxygen is introduced to a flame that has supplied its own controlled flow of oxygen for years. Now, the regulation cap has been blown off, and no replacement is within hundreds of miles.

The tale of Medusa, who remained steadfast in her devotion amidst the tempest of divine affections, I too have found myself in the midst of clouds. The world I have known and nurtured for over fifteen years, a sanctuary built by my own hands, has undergone a transformation that leaves me feeling unmoored and drifting out to sea for the first time since the destruction of Dionysia.

This upheaval, akin to the wrath of Poseidon, has stripped away the familiar compass points I've relied upon, challenging the very essence of my measured core. From a volunteer to a hospital worker, from a poet to a daydreamer, firefighter to minister, each role I've cherished now seems to be under siege by an unseen force, much like the Olympian army that Eros commands in allegory.

Yet, in this time of change, I am reminded that it is not the palace that defines one's world, but the spirit with which one builds and rebuilds amidst the ruins. I am compelled to seek solace in the resilience of those who have walked similar paths before me, but what leaves me in awe is that no one has walked a similar path. It's a path forged by two souls into the mystic.

Marc Antony and his time in the ornamented palaces of the Egyptian Nile delta. The sheer madness of his passion and the political intrigue that surrounded his life are subjects that I believe warrant a deeper exploration of the trail I seek with you, yet, it is a trail never traveled, not even by the most insane. As someone who has ventured into the uncharted territories of the Alaskan wilderness, I find a kindred spirit in the audacity of Marc Antony's pursuits of Cleopatra. His story is not just one of love and power but also a reflection of human ambition and its consequences. The accounts of his alliance and eventual conflict with Octavian, leading to the pivotal Battle of Actium, are as thrilling as any adventure I have embarked upon. Even the scent of the ancient perfumes that might have filled the air as he approached Cleopatra in his Roman strength and nudity is what I desire. Two powers colliding on an altar laid out by the Divine for the Gods to witness.

The profound connection I feel with God's nature and how it shapes my spiritual journey is a pantheistic view that sees divinity in every tree and stream, a belief that everything in the universe is interconnected. This perspective has brought me immense peace and understanding, and I wish to share this sense of unity with others. It's not always easy to convey the depths of such a worldview, especially when it requires a delicate balance of patience and self-control when I look into God's beauty. Now, I invite you to explore this world with me

It is difficult to articulate the depth of my thoughts, but I find myself compelled to reach out across the distance that separates us by time and distance. Of our inner cosmos, a celestial body whose gravity pulls at the very fabric of my being, I love you all. The nuances and complexities of our essence are like a symphony to which my soul cannot help but resonate, and the appreciation of seeing life in real-time is a blessing.

In my absence, I am akin to an accordion that you feel, compressing and expanding with a multitude of emotions. There is a profound power in the void I will have left behind, a current of longing that courses through me, relentless as the dawn that chases away Artemis.

I find myself at the precipice of patience, where the sea of time stretches out before me. My heart stands vigilant upon the shoreline where my heart found its home by this lighthouse, awaiting the moment when the tides of destiny will bring us together once more.

Truly Yours,
Daniel

RESURGAENCE

I once got lost on a beautiful day.
Absolutely crossed, nothing went my way.
Wandered in the woods, and I prayed to stay.
This is my home, in the middle of nowhere,
Where there is no melancholy gray.

Indiana Statehouse Rotunda
Indianapolis, Indiana
Photo by Daniel Wiita Livingston

Trapped In My Palace

These thick marble walls
Stand tall
In their glory.

A century of stories
Could be told in these halls
Of the days of grandeur.

As I wander through the dimly lit corridors, the weight of my solitude
presses down on me. Each step I take is a reminder of the opulence that
surrounds me, yet I feel more like a prisoner than a king. The grandeur
of my palace, with its towering ceilings and intricate carvings, only
serves to amplify my isolation.

In the Promenade, where once laughter and cheer filled the air, now
only silence reigns. The chandeliers, adorned with gold-leaf that catch
the faintest glimmer of light, hang like ghosts of a bygone era. I pause,
my reflection staring back at me from the polished marble floor, a
distorted image of a broken man who has everything yet nothing.

Memories flood my mind—lavish parties, esteemed guests, and the
intoxicating allure of power. But with power came responsibility, and
with responsibility came mistakes. The faces of those I wronged haunt
me, their eyes filled with disappointment and betrayal. I try to shake off
the guilt, but it clings to me like a second skin.

I make my way to the library, a sanctuary of knowledge and escape.
Shelves upon shelves of books line the walls, their spines worn from
years of use. I run my fingers along the titles, seeking solace in the
words of others. But even here, in this haven of wisdom, I find no
respite from my torment.

As the night deepens, I retreat to my private quarters surrounded by
photographs. This rocking chair of my grandfather's, draped in
luxurious fabrics, offers no comfort. I sit awake, staring at the faces of
those who once loved and adored me, now staring back in the flickering

15

flames from my fireplace. My mind is a whirlwind of regret and longing as I still adore them, and they loathe me in return. My bedroom, also a symbol of my success with my accolades hanging close, has become a shrine of friends that are no longer. They reach for me as if they wish for revenge. I run out of the room as the photographs yearn for my suffering.

A cage of solid walls constructed during a generation when things were built with care to last into the annals of time, is now a grave for my living existence. I run past the well-maintained flowers and into one of my night tenants. One of the few faces that knows my present state. I look at her. She looks at me. For a moment, a human connection that is then run down and bulldozed by fear. I turn and run up the staircase, my dress shoes clacking against the floor, reverberating in these halls.

I wish to run no more, but there is nowhere for my bones to rest in this palace. Desperation claws at my heart as I reach the highest tower. The wind howls through the open windows, a chilling reminder of my isolation. I step out onto the balcony, the city lights twinkling far below, indifferent to my plight.

My true prison is not this palace, but my own mind. These walls built by those who wished to protect myself are of no use to what is trapped beneath my epidermis. To break free from those I wronged and from myself is to throw myself over this balcony. For hours, I stand on this edge, peering down from my tearful eyes. I make the decision to jump to end the madness, but I contemplate for hours. My bravery turns to dread, and then defeat.

As the blue before the dawn breaks over the horizon, I feel a glimmer of hope that death won't be long. I turn away from the edge, ready to face whatever comes next. I journey down the stairs to my bedroom, for the faces of scorn to watch my exhaustion overtake my soul into slumber. This is my daily reprieve.

Happily Mad

Madness.
Embracing the madness.

Pain is so beautiful.
How one may control
With the grit of their teeth.
How else is weakness supposed to leave?

I frolic in the melancholy.
Bathe myself in the insanity.
Lather madly
Between the beads of water.
To swim in the essence of grief.

Who says that I am suffering?

Embracing instead of the usual brace,
Madness in laughter.
Blue glow afterglow.

Happily mad ever after.

Detroit Orchestra Hall
Detroit, Michigan
Photo by Daniel Wiita Livingston

Tears Whisper

From the Promenade, the flowers, delicate and fragile,
Are bestowed upon thee. As Osiris to his Isis,
I present these botanical hues,
That thy life may flourish and bloom.

Like Dionysus to his wife Ariadne,
In twilight's gentle embrace, they wander,
Through ancient groves and shadowed glens,
Their hearts entwined, a silent vow.

Beneath the moon's soft, silver gaze,
They tread the paths of myth and lore,
Where whispers of the past arise,
And time itself seems but a dream.

In quiet moments, hand in hand,
They find a world untouched by strife,
A sanctuary of the soul,
Where love endures, eternal, pure.

I miss you so deeply, tears seep through my stoic skin,
A silent sorrow, a quiet ache, where words cannot begin.
Tears bleed through my marrow, bones silently seep,
And sanity's white veil is lifted, revealing the depths of you, I keep.

In the shadows of my heart, your memory lingers still on our island,
A haunting presence, a void no time can fill.
Each moment without you, a silent scream within,
A testament to the love that flares, burning.

Teenage Smoker

In my teenage youth,
I would sit on the window-sill at night,
Listening to The Doors,
Smoking my pipe.

Every few moments,
A propeller plane would fly over,
Runway lights illuminating my presence,
While I sat there with my legs dangling.

Stolen cigarettes from my mother's purse,
I take another drag.
Smoke billowing into ice crystals
In the still winter dusk.
The hum of a distant highway,
Accompanied by the occasional siren.

Snowflakes lazily drifting
In a silver glow under Artemis.
Cold from the window frame biting into my skin,
The warmth of this cigarette,
A fleeting comfort from the blowing wind
Stress external,
Some within.

It's frosty nights in Michigan that I like.

Bob Seger playing over a left-on radio in someone's garage.
Red and blue police lights glow
On the streets down below.

I sit here.
Meek.
Quiet.
Calm.
Breaking the law from high above.

My existence in the dark.
Tranquil serenity in this solitude.
Safe above after altitude.

Coming into present reality,
I miss that world, knowing I can never go back.
Memories flickering like an old film reel of a world that no
longer exists.
Only defiance and rebellion left in a soul,
Withering in decay.

In this suit and tie,
I dream of that world.
The world of being invincible.
High above the Earth,
Perched in my nest,
Smoking a stolen cigarette before rest.

Eyes Waiting
Detroit, Michigan
Photo by Daniel Wiita Livingston

10 Lines w/ You

In stillness of our days, we tire of waiting,
Our hourglass, weary, fades with sandy shores' erosion.
A silent stir within, a movement faint,
No longer do we chase hollow dreams of others' pen.
We rise, determined, in this fleeting hour,
The world around us trembles, quakes with power.
My heart, it bleeds beneath the weight of time,
Sleepless, restless, for our dreams to meet.
Together, we shall steer this world anew,
Towards paths iridescent, bright with hue.

Untitled

In yonder vale, where shadows softly creep,
A man of years, with heart in sorrow steeped,
Did wander forth, his spirit bruised and torn,
A knife cut deep by love's cruel hand, to solitude was borne.

His lover's touch, once balm to weary soul,
Now distant memory, a gaping hole.
For in his mind, the echoes of the past,
Did haunt his days, a storm that ever lasts.

With a heavy heart, he sought the countryside,
Where nature's peace and quiet might abide.
Amongst the hills, where heather blooms so fair,
He found a refuge from his deep despair.

In solitude, 'neath ancient oaks he lay,
And pondered life, as night gave way to day.
The whispers of the wind, the brook's soft song,
Did soothe his heart, and made his spirit strong.

He penned his thoughts in verses pure and true,
Of pain and loss, and love's sweet residue.
Yet in those lines, a spark began to grow,
A flame of self, that he had yet to know.

Through days and nights, in nature's calm embrace,
He learned to love himself, to find his place.
No longer bound by chains of past regret,
He forged a path, his heart no longer set.

In yonder vale, where shadows softly creep,
A man reborn, from sorrow's deepest sleep.
With love for self, his spirit now did soar,
A journey ended, yet begun once more.

An Ocean of Faith

From the harsh toil of Winter's wrath,
Lay half of the landing party,
With lovers bereft,
Their breath mingling with the icy wind,
Faces etched with what hope is left.

With Native generosity,
Corn planted seeds of curiosity,
In the frost-kissed soil of a new world.

Today, I look into this puddle,
Reflecting on our shared legacy,
The pilgrim stares back up at me,
Eyes blue, mirroring the vast Atlantic sea,
A silent testament to you and me.

As churches close their doors,
Like these evaporating puddles that shrivel,
Our light lives within us,
Guiding those who need the love of Jesus,

Once again, our church doors will open
With the work we do for tomorrow.
As they did all those centuries ago,
Where Pilgrim's beauty
is sacrificed through Scriptures' glow,
For a hurting world to see God's mercy
Eternally bestowed.

Detroit Institute of Arts – North Lawn
Detroit, Michigan
Photo by Daniel Wiita Livingston

In Nature, Time

The dame I desire lies on an island,
While I stand on the shore of my freshwater lore.
My dear enchanted forested peninsula,
How many tears have you soaked in your soil
Before I dropped to my knees at Hades' door?

Crickets sing their last serenade as autumn rolls.
Quietly, I sit solemnly beneath the celestial heavens,
Gazing towards hydrogen light years to their solar core.
If only the stars could talk about all I've told them and shout.

My dear, one moment filled with joy,
And the next with longing.
Poseidon's jealousy keeps you on a surrounded island
With white-squalled seas.

Why?
Does he wish me dead?
Does he desire my suffering?
Does he wish for me to shake the mountains?

Why must one swim in pain as if a leaf without the Sun?
If only Father Time and Mother Nature could intertwine,
To have her near the heartbeat within my caged madness.
Beating drums and frenzy ecstasy beneath the heartbreak of
distance.

I feel her on my skin, caressing my chest.
Her scent on my shoulders causing my eyelids to cease the light.
With dying days, winter will be near and withered, at best.
My soul will sink for another hour.
To wait, my conscience shall be dreadfully devoured.

Rose Rapture

Roses appear at my door.

Forevermore, I adore the embodiment of your essence,
As the effervescence of my soul illuminates with this floral bouquet.
I clasp onto your fish with my hand, bring it to my muzzle,
And reminisce about memories of our abode.

Gathering my day from a distant land,
I make my way to the Sacred Shores.
There, I lay esteemed and daydream of the dame
I wish to be laying near Heaven's door.

By ancient royal decree, I make my way towards the beacon of Hope.
Gulls greet the familiar gentleman standing along the shores.
Here, I dream and let go...

I approach the lighthouse where our origin was solidified in the annals of
time.
While the wilderness witnessed our hearts exposed to the stars,
The gulls swarmed overhead to greet me with their calls.
Step by step, I come closer to the marble pillar that blinks on the edges of
time,
Where the edge of the world resides. I cast my gaze into the vast open
water.

Northeast, towards Ireland, where stories are being made on the Emerald
Isle.
Stories of the woman who touched my heart from thousands of miles away.
Before I could utter a prayer, this is what Persephone had to say...

"Two rainbows from One World...Under Michigan Stars.
Two chipmunks with a mosaic over theirs.
Two youthful swans carefree to where the wind blows.
Two does' grazing while dazzled in your mindful maze.
Two hours until time ends and after death, it begins all over again.
Close your eyes and dream of the day,
Of the three words you have always wanted to say."

Once Was a World Not to Miss

In the midst of electronic hums from my labor,
I stare through the windowless walls knowing what lies beyond.
Fond artworks to bond
The spirit
With the soul.

Before I go,
I pay my toll
To cross the River of Styx.

Is my primordial soul beckoning to go back to a world that no longer
exists?
Because, I don't feel bad for the world I no longer miss.

I used to be once,
And now once was.

A whole mystical world laid undiscovered beneath my bridge.
We can only marvel at what once was,
And chart into the unknown.

Hoist the bowlines
And unfurl the sails.
There is a fairytale unfolding
From the corners of Mother Earth.

One death.
One birth.
Another death,
Continual rebirth.

My compass spins
As I sail into the quiet abyss.
Don't look for me
If I become domestically missed.

Let me live in this lust
While the moonlight insanely grins.

Hyatt Regency Indianapolis
Indianapolis, Indiana
Photo by Daniel Wiita Livingston

North Loft

Up the stairs where labyrinthine paths wind,
A century of souls, in wonderment confined.
This place, once called "my mobile office, nest,"
Now near the Promenade, where I find rest.

In airless chambers, where breath doth flee,
Each touch of thine hand, a grasp on me.
Above the Royal Court, on secret floors I tread,
Gazing down, pondering the night's dread.

Interwoven 'twixt steam pipes and vents,
To the trail's end, where my journey's spent.

Untitled

Amidst the toils and labors of the day,
In moments of respite, a bittersweet daydream.

Holding you, your head on my chest, my place of solace.
A calm, relentless grace ignited by a single thought,
Brings me back to where you belong.

Eyes closed, protection and care, love and grace,
In the cold, frigid wind's beauty, we find our peace.

The Promenade

Sitting upon this teal velvet bench,
I gaze upon the ancient marble floor where once our feet did
meet.
You, with a delicate hand, played with your hair,
And my veins and arteries did swell with the lingering scent of
your perfume in the air.

My arms, though empty,
Feel your presence near,
As if you were still here.

The Promenade, long in its length,
Echoes your voice that I miss so dear.
From jazz to Belle Isle,
You shall not be forgot'.

Denali Seat by the Creek
Denali, Alaska
Photo by Daniel Wiita Livingston

Privatum

Sedentarium in prato ubi juventutem meam exegi;
Somnium cum ea nocte volantem.

Insano amore.

Somnio te dum immersus insania.
Cum luna propius horizontem deprimitur,
Schedae eius recedunt et fiunt terrae.

Descende in collum tuum mordeo.
Lacrimam teneo amori meo.

Insano amore.
Volo te intus sentire.

Pueri sumus is mundo ridentes
Te clamare volo.

Expando crura tua,
Cotidie magis sentio.

Vinum tuum in calicem meum.
Sicut pellem tuam super meam.

Ode to Academia

Academia, the jungle of papers.
The wilder-vines of pages
Endless books, by brooks that school, crafting wisdom
Forgiven by those who perhaps should not.

All this time not forgot'
Is the Dame o' Green
On the Isle swiftly not
Within reach
Being taught at Trinity
That I shall beseech.

Unforeseen.
Not Forgot'.

Untitled

In the stillness of the nocturnal blue hour,
Beneath the celestial canopy, stars of the moon hidden by oaks,
I find myself enraptured by the profound beauty of this darkness.
The twilight of Helios' crown, with its gentle luminance,
Heralds the dawn of Aurora, casting a delicate glow upon the world.

As a devoted admirer of the dusk and its mysterious muse,
My Ophelia, virtuous and fervent soul, who turns from the world;
Fall into my arms to feel your embrace.

I yearn for your claws to dig into my flesh in pure ecstasy,
Scraping my skin under your nails.
I need to feel you fade into me.

Kenai Peninsula
Kenai Peninsula, Alaska
Photo by Daniel Wiita Livingston

Black Reverie

In somnolent voyages amidst astral seas,
I rouse this morn with fervid blaze,
'Neath cotton's taut embrace, my spirit frees,
To traverse the labyrinthine starry maze.

Betwixt the Moon and scintillant stars,
I quest for thee 'mongst celestial tsars,
With spears honed and Buddha's ascension,
My tongue doth trace thy silken extension.

As Artemis pirouettes with Helios resplendent,
In crepuscular embrace, they gyrate and entwine,
Yet Helios pursues her into the nocturnal firmament,
As aurora's first luminescence heralds the diurnal design.

I supplicate to be enraptured, in spirits' tenebrous clasp,
To realms where umbra and conflagration hold dominion,
Engulfed by the susurrations of temporal and spatial expanse,
Diving into infernal chariots, where reveries disintegrate.

Forget-Me-Not, M'dame

In the whisper of the leaves along the island ground,
The song of the breeze, nature speaks in its gentle sound.

In forests, fields, and ancient Egyptian stones,
The river's flickering Alaskan dance
Under the epitaphs are native bones.

Denali's mountain's might,
Cassiopeia's stars pierce the velvet night,
Each element, gold and quartz
A story weaves with you among us in thistle thorns.
In the whisper of the leaves,
The sunset makes for morning dew,
Artemis casts her silver hue.

In every season, life renews.
Death. Burial. Resurrection.
A symphony of countless blues.
From the smallest trillium to the tallest Taiga tree,
A howling wolf's beauty, wild and free,
A snowy canvas painted white, pure in grace,
A timeless, sacred, wondrous place.

To Anchorage, and to Seward we shall roam,
Beneath the Arctic sky, we wander to Nome.
The Northern Lights, a celestial dance,
In your company, I'll take the chance.

Together we'll witness the heavens' glow,
In hues of green, blue, and indigo.
A gift from the cosmos, a sight to see,
Under the starlit canopy.
Utqiagvik, just you and me.

BRAIN DAMAGE POEM!

I'm still here. Stillness. Alone.
Paranoia as if they are watching.
Waiting to pounce.
Incessant beeping.

Beep. Beep. Beeping.

Madness. Grabbing my cranium while wearing another security
jacket.
Whose jacket? I don't know.
Grabbing my head while walking down the Promenade.
Where am I going? I don't know.

On camera. Wandering the hallways. Holding my head. Screaming.
Talking to the voices.
She's there. She's here.
While everyone comes to devour,
She does not call me weak in my desperate hour.
I have been strong for too long.
I only see weakness.
She finds me strong,
In my meekness.
I'll grab the amulet.
However, I lost it in the fog.
I wish you were here,
She is....
.... right here.
.... With me.

Sitting in the dark wondering what the next minute will bring,
Full of fear. I hate fear.
I don't know how to wear fear.
I wish I could give it to the two deer.
On the island.

41

They kept me company when she was not near.
I always think people are going to leave.
They do.

All my friends left today.
Checked out, all because I'm gray.
Not her. She stayed.
Wearing blue. How true. So true.
I want to be better,
So we can again play.
Dreams at my fingertips,
But the matter in my brain is gray. Paralyzed.
With her, I am wanting to play.
I can't. But I desire to get better so I can.
Thoughts with the endless pelting.
"Ye without sin, cast the first stone."
It's raining rocks on me. Boulders. Mountains.
And the mountain caps.

I want to be better.

I want to be with her.

In Alaska, Ireland, Paris.....

With her!

Untitled

Remember, remember the 5th of November.

Sitting in the garage after being woken up by Johnny Law and his brother.
Both gentlemen are friendly.

One officer from Schoolcraft, who went to the same Academy as me, next door.

Work too much, I'm a fool.
Work too little, I'm a bum.
Damned if I do.
Damned if I don't.

Fears validated. In reality, I am loved.
In my head, full of fear. Why?
Why is it anytime that I heal that I have foes pushing me back?

It's a warm night. Crickets are chirping, and it must be in the 50s.

Sitting in this lawn chair with a long sleeve gray shirt and black running pants.

I'm polishing my shoes in front of my car.

Pilgrim Monument
Provincetown, Massachusetts
Photo by Daniel Wiita Livingston

The Blue Sea of Tranquility

In the quietude of twilight's tender embrace,
Where shadows dance upon the Promenade walls,
You linger in my mind.
A feather falls from the sky
And into your hand.
Descending from the whirlwind heavens high,
Descended in whispered surrender
To be embraced in your palm
As if my heart had fallen for you.
To you.
Through you.
To be with you.

Your reverence to Artemis
Has my heart sinking into the darkness
Of the fathomless abyss,
A celestial madness longing entwined with despair,
As the stars whisper secrets of forgotten dreams
Of a life I dare not,
Shall not return.

The moon, a sentinel guard in the night's expanse,
Watches over our fleeting moments,
Each sigh a testament to unspoken truths,
Each glance of your eyes is a brush with the ethereal.

The Blue Sea of Tranquility.
Once illuminated by gas-lit lamps
Now being illuminated by the blue before dawn.
Helios' rays shine upon us.

You, I, and The Blue`   Sea of Tranquility.

Denali Glacier Flight
Denali, Alaska
Photo by Daniel Wiita Livingston

Arctic Snow

In dreams of snowy Arctic night,
We dwell within our A-frame bright,
Where flick'ring flames in hearth's warm glow,
Cast shadows dancing, soft and slow.

As dusk descends, the world turns black,
A velvet cloak, no light to track;
Yet in this dark, our spirits soar,
On whispered winds, to distant ocean shores.

The frost-kissed air coats the clovers divine,
In Artemis' stillness, hearts and souls entwine;
With every sigh, the night ignites the moonlight,
In love's embrace, our dreams take flight.

Trodden South

Whilst slumbering in my hotel,
My soul did depart my being within a dream.
As I trotted down the hallway,
Silent laughter ensued, for I dared not scream.

None need witness my escape,
Nor hear my footfalls in this late hour.
I approached the desk clerk with curiosity, inquiring,
"Which way should I go?"
The desk clerk replied,
"Go to Ridgeport, if you wish to know."

Without fumble or folly, I slipped out the door,
In my maddening jollity.
Westward I went, through the old township of my birth.
Once called Superior, now Ypsilanti.
Once a rebel,
Now a vigilante.

Tilting south out of the Concrete Jungle,
Down Old Chicago Road.
On to trails once trodden by natives,
Through the Irish Hills where spirits spoke.

Through whispers, I weaved and trotted
To Ridgeport, where childhood memories are blotted.

Coldwater, Auburn, Fort Wayne,
Through the flat farms of Indiana,
Through the remnants of the 1776 reign.

Muncie, Marion, Anderson, Indianapolis, Martinsville,
Bloomington.

"Should you lose your way, seek out the portly gentleman
Adorned with a corn straw hat and a blade of grass between his
teeth.
His abode will be on the left, marked by a dog, a rocking chair, and
a shotgun.
He will offer guidance, but tread carefully, maintain your
composure,
And exhibit politeness in these parts.
The local men may emerge unexpectedly, and you must remain
vigilant."

Trotting the final leg, everything became familiar.
This was the beginning of "The Woods" of my childhood,
Away from the Taiga.

The woods where mosquitoes form the fog,
And the fog is cut with a butter knife.

Stifling heat, deafening locusts.
Habitual sweat, irritable focus.
Through the rolling hills of Appalachia, the farmer tills and turns.
Fuel and fire, the pile of leaves burned.

I reached the hilltop of my childhood play,
And turned to my translator, who had this to say...

"Escort the lady of your dreams to the cave,
Where she may meet your family.
Engage in conversations about love and conspiracy theories,
And revel in steadfast affection and merriment."

Indiana War Memorial
Indianapolis, Indiana
Photo by Daniel Wiita Livingston

Unforgiven Decay in My Imperfections

I am not a perfect man by any means,
Stoic without; artistic within.

My calcified bones, their organs surround,
In the decay of its plight, death is found.

With family and friends, I embrace the end,
In shadows of twilight, where souls transcend.

If I might unveil my madness,
In verses fair and true,
I capture our shared poetry,
This day, my gift to you.

Thy Serenade of Bells

Thy serenade of bells, a freedom's chime,
That rings within my life, a tune sublime.
The fire that breathes into my roots so deep,
Thy trembling, lustful breath, my soul doth keep.

My liberty breathes into my soul,
Doth keep me from the brink of madness, where I weep.
Madness, my sole liberty, is found
Within thy womb, where love and life abound.

Thou hast a wondrous missive awaiting thine eyes,
To peruse at thy leisure.
How I yearn to awaken beside thee!
Yet, as the morn doth break and our forms remain apart,

I share with the floral splendor that doth grace this day.
In every step I take through this hallowed space,
My thoughts pay homage to the noble dame afar.
The dame whom I long to behold,
Amidst the blossoms that bloom with thee.

Ever thine!

Untitled

In the quiet aftermath of day's end,
I assume my vigil amidst silent halls,
Till twilight's gentle embrace.

The guardians of the day have departed,
And I, with careful hand, secure each portal,
Ensuring solitude remains within.

Stepping out, I seal myself in,
A sentinel in the stillness,
No soul in sight, no whisper near.

Here, in this hushed art sanctuary, I cherish moments fleeting,
Tears fall, smiles bloom, desires linger.

McCormick's Creek State Park – Mushroom
Spencer, Indiana
Photo by Daniel Wiita Livingston

The Pond

Down the path of laden Maple and Ash leaves,
A young boy, trotting down the hill through thick Hoosier woods to play.
Black crows and vultures circle overhead,
Seeking the mice I killed, now laid for dead.

Clouds blow over with their billowing grays,
Passing by the days of my youth.
Sticks and thorns clasp onto cotton cloths to stay,
To the pond I go where the beavers play.

Building the dam from giant oak trees,
I sit on the edge of the water, listening to the last of the bees,
Buzzing their final decree.

The limestone hills stand guard, silent and tall,
While the cave whispers secrets of old.
A stream flows gently, a gift from the cave,
Where beavers' dam has formed a pond, serene and brave.

Reflections of the sky dance on the water's face,
Ripples from frogs spreading memories of a simpler place.
Here, in the heart of nature's embrace,
I find solace, a moment of grace.

Untitled

I was to die, and be reborn again.

I died, and painfully returned.

Perpetually, I wish to die with you

With pains of rebirth are nevermore.

With you, 'could this have happened.

Returning, our next sunset, be painted blue.

Judge and Prosecutors

Prisoner of my own mind.
Mental struggle.
Front-line leaning rest has me ill
In this trash-ridden urban jungle.

Youth generated.
City bus to the bus station
From the Library of Alexander,
To the slums of the Bronx, Harlem
And the chambers of the United Nations.
To the King of Solomon all the way to the Book of Psalms.
Shoot me to death with spikes through Jesus' palms.

What are the implications
Of a young mind
Fed to the swines of prosecutors
For thought crimes
Paid for by the District Attorneys
For anti-government rhymes.

Detained for narrating
And rearranging words poetically.
Straining my brain
In the crosshairs to be carried on a gurney,
A justice system to squeeze the young mind
Of the knowledge,
Blood-stained pages of King Solomon.

Ronald Wilson Reagan
Ronald - Six
Wilson - Six
Reagan - Six
Does Satan need any explanation?

America is in pain, insane.
Sleep-walkers, shadows creeping outside my window
CIA, ATF night stalkers.
Shadows, ghosts of Herbert Walker
And his leftover hungry crows.

Insomnia, paranoia of red dots through my window.
I'm getting sick of this tremulous surveilled ghetto.
Did so many have to die in Manhattan that day?
America is asleep while I am on the Apparatus,
Bullets flying to the fire scene.
Where is the gratis
For those on 9/11.
Did they make it to Hell or Heaven?

Thank you, Uncle Sam, for my taxed paycheck.
To operate secret operations.
While I am on Hell's Red Engine,
Lights and Sirens.

Driving a spike through my brain to make a fraction.
I am calling on the people of these United States
To take up "two arms"
And a call to action.

Untitled

My heart has been stolen, but it does not feel taken hostage.
Swooning and speechless from our conversation late into the night.
Now, my breath gets taken away in the morning, but suffocation I
do not feel.
Enamored, and love and compassion that has no words, my heart
can only reveal.

Each day, at OUR Art Palace, I seek this painting's gentle grace,
To find my calm, to dream in tranquil space.
Beneath the shade, where whispering breezes play,
Through trees that sway, their leaves in soft array.

The flowers dance, as I in shadows lie,
'Neath nature's giants, reaching to the sky.
Now, with you, my love, this vision I embrace,
We rest, we read, and love in this sweet place.

The flowers dance, as I in shadows lie,
'Neath nature's giants, reaching to the sky.
Now, with you, my love, this vision I embrace,
We rest, we read, and love in this sweet place.

Alaskan Hotel
Juneau, Alaska
Photo by Daniel Wiita Livingston

Love is Dead

We made love on the island hew.
Watching the sunset with its final blue.
Your love cast to the Emerald Isle
All the while I cry.
Who cares. I sigh.

A man cannot be loved without conditions.
Nothing ever comes to fruition.
Romantically doomed.
Whatever is left of us,
I take the broom
And sweep the dust
Of whatever lust
We laid.

Romance is dead.
The unbridled killed chivalry with Cupid's bullets filled with lead.
To fall in love. How could I have been so stupid?

Love is Dead.

Slip My Fingers

In twilight's gentle, fading light,
Where shadows dance and stars ignite,
My heart, with scars unseen,
Bears silent wounds from quarrels keen.

Beneath Artemis's pale, silver glow,
Where memories of love and embrace still flow,
A mind besieged by echoes past,
In dreams where peace and love are seldom cast.

The island willow weeps beside the channel stream,
Its branches brush a haunted dream,
In my loss and cries of pain,
In fields where love was in vain.

Yet in the silence of night,
There lies hope, a glimmer bright,
That healing touch to my heart may find a way,
And dawn will bring a brighter day.

Onto Escanaba

To the snowy white north,
Lieutenant Dan and Cat in the Hat,
We're on to Escanaba, with a suitcase and a hat.

For the journey lives on and the imagination is wild,
Through the moose-ridden woods, where the snow is neatly piled.

With a hop and a skip, and a plane in the sky,
They flew over Lake Michigan, miles high, oh my, oh my!

The wind it did howl, and the snow it did fall,
But nothing could stop them, no nothing at all.

For the story will be written, for their lives to play,
In the land of the north, where the moose loves to stay.

With laughter and cheer, and adventures so grand,
Lieutenant Dan and the Cat to Escanaba, in this snowy white land.

Washington Mushrooms
Spokane, Washington
Photo by Daniel Wiita Livingston

Dim Electric

In the dim glow of flickering screens, my colleagues lie as shadows on the floor,
While I, sleepless, etch my poetic thoughts into the light,
The weight of words pressing against my weary eyes, bags heavy.

You draw near, a presence electric, my heart thrumming against the cage of my ribs,
Anticipation swelling, as if I am reborn in this moment, ready to be undone by your touch.

Night deepens, and dreams unfurl—roses bloom in the streets of Ireland,
Your voice a soft echo against my ear, a melody that cradles my thoughts,
Imagining the dream to lift you, to carry you through the streets of Dublin.

Outside, the dawn whispers, birds heralding a new day,
While my fingers weave through the silk of your hair, lost in the warmth of our shared silence.

Only death can still the ache of longing, but here, in this fleeting hour,
We exist, unbound by time from afar.

Delayed in Escanaba

As the sun pulls below the horizon,
The fireball waits to spread illumination.
With frustration,
I traverse south on these eagle wings.

Over Lake Michigan,
Detroit-bound.
Wheels of our airplane frozen to the ground.

Escanaba,
Land of wintry bluster and frozen sound.
I will not frown if South is where I do not go down.

Jazzy Nights

Heavenly nocturnal Motown streets.
Brown-eyed dame.
Jazzy beats.
Starlit by Dionysus' flame.

Heartfelt calm within a caged chest.
Jailed by beauty behind bars.
Moon rising over the horizon to crest
And down in the shadows of stars.

Wanderer of the Last Frontier.
Not so alone in the mystic.
After all, the kind are about.

Awoken from sleep, eroding fear
Of the one who's altruistic.
The one chipping away at my doubt.

Pavilion at Riverfront Park
Spokane, Washington
Photo by Daniel Wiita Livingston

Is This...

Emerald Isle
All the while
Thoughts of wild dreams.
Eroding away on Hadrian's Wall
Twist, turn, a fire now burns.

Conflagrating.

My heart, a vibrant nation
With its armies now awoken.
Rome will not fall.
The fire stoked
Within a stirred soul.

A feeling not accustomed.
A disruption to my hermetism.

Breath falling away
In reverence.

Untitled

Along the sacred shores of our youth,
We lay there and listened to each other's whispers under the
Milky Way.

Two Dionysian souls greeting the dusk like last night's
welcomed friend.

"Let's no longer pretend, my dear," I say to her softly.

Her skin, so soft.
Cocooning our spirits against the breeze.
A rebirth from the last death.
Criminal to be this eased.

fLuX PoEm

A
IRELAND
WITH
E. E. CUMMINGS
READING   S
A   BELLE N
OUT   PROMENADE
DUBLIN   W
NIMPH   Y
G'MORNING   E
A
MISSING-HER

Alaskan Flower
Seward, Alaska
Photo by Daniel Wiita Livingston

Mountain Flower

Delicate in hues,
Bouncing down with white and blues.
Forget-Me-Not in the Last Frontier.
A soldier this high in altitude,
Cold blustery winds bringing tears.
Miss me until forgot.
Climb these rocks
As far to the sky.
The air thin this high.

The edelweiss to the German,
Forget-Me-Not to the American.
The dead in the sermon.

Whispers of the Heart

I cannot describe the feelings that stir within me this morning.
If I could grasp a few fleeting thoughts, they would weave in and out of
emotions—a delicate dance between longing and courage.

Love, elusive and rare, has been my silent adversary.
Yet now, my sword rests in its sheath, and my arms,
Like open tarnished wings from war, await your arrival.

At ease, we sway—two souls entwined.
Tranquil moments stretch into eternity, each heartbeat echoing our
shared ache.
I miss you as much as each exhale longs for oxygen.

How I yearn for slow dances beneath the moon's tender gaze on Irish
streets.
Outdoors, where the forest wears its green and black madness,
And nostalgia floats like a silken veil among the clouds.

My daydreams, once solitary, now crave your company.
Today, there is nothing more than to have you woven into the fabric of
my world—
A whispered promise, a love story that dances across the Earth.

May your heart find solace in these words,
And may your day be filled with the magic of longing and possibility.
I ache. I smile. I take the seat belt off of this roller coaster
So I may stand up and leap over the next hill.
Pardon me while I crave for you to crash into me with reckless force.

Consort of Osiris, Third of January

From my netherworld abode,
I abhor your absence.

Upon my throne,
I gaze at your vacant seat.
From my bed, my bones wither, lifeless.

I endeavor to articulate the fervent desire simmering within my veins.
The agony of your absence, yearning to caress your soul.
Your breasts I wish to lay
My sexual desires, my arborvitae loses control.

Within the breast, a beastly roar doth rise,
A creature fierce, with stone-like heart and guise.
Its fervent wish, to ravage her and to claim,
In depths of his passion, seeks his fiery aim.

In the depths of my sickly madness,
I traverse the darkened road, forlorn,
To dwell within my shadowed cave,
Where I yearn to lure thee, my dear Isis,
That we may inherit the Underworld's throne.

To share a world with thee, my heart's delight,
A feast to savor thy beauty's radiant light.
To make love by Egyptian torches' glow,
Crawling towards each other, in lustful throes.

Reflections at Dawn
Detroit, Michigan
Photo by Daniel Wiita Livingston

Untitled

I miss you.
Your heart swims away to your Isle Kingdom.
You're still here, beating within.

Standing by the lake while the sun wanes.
Wind blowing through your hair.
I ache with you not in my arms, protected.

Rest your head on my chest while I slide my fingers through your hair.

My swan, hold close while I bind your wounds.
Rest easy next to me tonight.
Let Pan come to take your dreams to flight.

Turmoil in the Streets

Blood in the streets of the town of Mount Clemens.
Riots in the streets in the town of Ann Arbor.
Chaos on the streets in the city of Detroit.

Death. Burial. Resurrection.
Death. Burial. Resurrection.

That's all you ever hear from the pews, but does anyone know what that feels like?

Death. Burial. Resurrection.

Everyone lives a single life as if it were a long day.

"You only live once," they say.
To have innocence ripped from you, like Persephone taken to the Underworld by Hades.

Unceremoniously, life is smoldering into dust. Thrown in a pit to burn for the pigs to eat the remnants by dawn.

Death. Burial. Sunset. Dusk.

The blue before the sunrise. The light before the dawn. First remnants of a new day beginning.
Still winds. Silent air. Fog blanketing the horizon. Deer tiptoeing through the brush.

Trifolium to oxidize.

Alive. Again, reborn. Eyes opened. Enlightened.
With you standing along the shoreline. Hair flowing. My heart from ashes, reborn.
Now, adorned.

The love I adore is to die again. With you, there is no sadness or mourn.
To die with you is my honor. Valiantly, I'll never waste a day somber.
Hold me shoulder tight while I embrace you with my arms.
Artemis will be with us again. With you, my ghost ship is moored.

Your Sunday Empathy

Your empathy and awareness of traumas past,
Speak volumes of your growth, steadfast.
The chain of events you have overcome,
To build this beautiful dame, where once was none.
In the Promenade, where fate did find,
Your perseverance, a strength of mind.

Not projecting fears onto others' hearts,
A strength I admire, where resilience starts.
In a mindless world, detached yet near,
Most do not think, nor change, I fear.
Too busy as voyeurs in life's grand play,
Yet in this abyss, your foundation lay.

Your beauty felt, your soul profound,
In you, a steadfast strength is found.
Through repetitive resilience, you stand tall,
In a world so mindless, you heed the call.
Your beauty, a beacon in the night,
Guiding souls with your radiant light.

The Pyramids
Indianapolis, Indiana
Photo by Daniel Wiita Livingston

Are You Even Real?

Are you even real? I ponder in the night,
Reaching for celestial stars so bright.
You've turned my life, once plain and clear,
Into something surreal, beyond the sphere.

In cosmic dust where czars have tread,
Your presence lingers, fills my head.
A wondrous dream, a mystic flight,
In realms of shadow and of light.

Dreaming of you here in Detroit,
I plan my voyage to the universe in your eyes,
Where stars whisper secrets and the cosmos lies.
In the depths of your gaze, I find my way,
A celestial journey, night and day.

She is of the Earth

She is of the Earth,
And she found her calm harbor
Behind my gated heart.

She is gone days, weeks, months,
Steadfast, I remain headstrong
Because I know where she belongs.

Eyes closed, her breath rolling away on my skin.
Slowing.
Still.
Soft.
Gilded.
Gleaming.

Slumbering on her breasts
I say goodbye to my domestic land.
Giant lakes come to a still.
Waves silence on the shores.

Our sun sets among the abodes.
Yellow.
Orange.
Red.
Crimson.
Blue.
Black.

The venomous beast now sleeps.
Breathing in, I smell her.

The waves come from the shore

And weave through her hair.

Crickets.
Chirping.
Birds' last serenade.

Armies gather under the cover of night.
Starlit and struck, boats loaded for the flight.

The Manitou Light blinks.
Once and then twice.
The signal to sail eastward is bestowed.
A bare chest burns bright.
Fervently
The fire is luminous inside.

I can feel Boudica distantly.
Drum-beat pulse.
Quelled is my monstrous temperance
With her gentle touch.

She is of the Earth,
And she found her calm harbor
Behind my gated heart.

McCormick's Creek State Park – Fire Tower
Spencer, Indiana
Photo by Daniel Wiita Livingston

What is Love?

Madness.
Desire.
Fire.

Love is the tempest to my soul.
Outside in this snowy cold,
Smoking a bowl,
I cry.

All my life,
I was told that there is no better feeling than love.
To love is to die.

Strife to life.
Grief to affirmative relief.
I am a man,
Kept company by his own plans.
My dreams wither in the quicksand,
While my admiration takes its last stand.
Snakes packaged neatly in cans.

I close my eyes for reprieve.

25 Years Later

I've always been able to escape them.

Outwit.
Out charm.
Out run.
Out eat.
Outperform.

I can never be in their grasp.
They would get their hands on me,
But I would always find a crack to slide through.

Kept fit.
Kept clean.
Kept sliding through the cracks.

Padded rooms with all the pills,
They can never get me to stay.
Never lock and step.

No one understood.
No one understands.

Then…

Then you crashed through my thick artistic walls…

…and became part of the plan.

10-7

Under the clouds of pastel grey; upon your wings, death's slay.
First view starting the day.
Last view leaving abode.

The art you create shines light in all of my dark cracks.
While I float among the "enthusiasts" who strut their game.
My bubble consists of Etta James and Dame.

At the place of my labor, I turn this corner, and open you to another
world.
Promenade, the spot where I am immersing myself.

The Dove in the Belly, read from my chair.
Out for my pocket, the eye that stares.
A heart stolen from abroad.
A heart's decay, Pan applauds.

Statue of Liberty
Liberty Island, New York
Photo by Daniel Wiita Livingston

10-8

In the stillness of this moment, your words pierce my heart like a
gentle arrow,
Awakening a dormant passion within.
As if touched by a ghostly muse, I feel a surge of longing,
A thirst for the ethereal beauty you embody.
You are not a mere pursuer of hearts, but a celestial being
Whose presence ignites a fleeting yet divine fire,
Leaving an indelible mark on my soul.
In your embrace, I find a love that burns with the intensity of a
thousand stars,
Wild and untamed, yet profoundly tender.
Your care is a shield, your love a light,
Guiding me through the darkest night.
In your arms, I find my home, my love.

My colleague departs the hallowed IOC.
Breath quickens, down below grows taut with dread.
Heart pounds fiercely, seeking to break free.
At this moment, emotions are widespread.
Cum seeping from Dragon's head.

The Muse in the Theatre

In the realm of academic discourse, the dream is likened to the sound of the Dionysian theatre buried beneath the wilderness, where memory and reality intertwine. Casting grapevines into the wilderness, I yearn to reconnect with a primordial nature, an attempt to reclaim a dominion lost to the annals of time. This journey led me to the Sacred Promenade, a place resonant with the echoes of my youth, where the boundaries between the past and present are as ethereal as the realm itself.

Upon emerging from a deep vortex, I found myself within the walls of an ancient theater I once knew. The once vibrant hub stood silent, its blue velvet seats and historic wooden stage enveloped in a serene stillness that spoke volumes of a long-ago storied past. In its quiet abandonment, it was a canvas on which the echoes of past performances lingered, inviting a reflection on the countless tales that had unfolded on its stage. The air seemed heavy with the weight of dramatic pauses and resonant monologues, all now faded into a hushed reverence for the art that once lived here.

The organ's melodies once filled the air with life, touching the hearts of all who were fortunate enough to hear its harmonious tunes. Now, as we walk on this stage, the silence is profound, the past vibrancy that once echoed off these walls. The dust that gently settles upon the organ's keys and pipes shrouds the cherished memories like a delicate veil.

In my musings, I stand amidst the remnants of a bygone era, enveloped by the vestiges of joy and life that have now succumbed to the quietude of abandonment. A contemplation on whether there are others who share this affinity for spaces that time has forgotten, those who find solace in the stillness of environments once vibrant with existence. The essence of this experience blurs the lines between the dream state and waking reality, unraveling the threads that weave the stage curtains of my past with the beauty found within decay and dereliction.

As I try to understand the world around me, the stillness and the desolate space, there is life. The spiders and scarabs that have made a home amidst the shadows are a symbol of resilience and continuity. Even in the quietest moments, life persists, adapting and awaiting the opportunity to emerge once again.

Beneath the grand stage, an unexpected protagonist awoke from her slumber. With her mindful agility, she scurried up the Emerald staircase, her mission clear and its presence unnoticed by the one-person crowd. The rafters, usually silent and still, became the runway for this tiny creature's urgent errand.

As she stood atop the stage looking down from the catwalks, a profound sense of her perspective entered into my heart. It was in this moment of quiet reflection, amidst the unusual flurry in my veins, the fire instilled inside of my soul burned its ashes down to become crystal clear.

While she turned the stage lights blue...

This fleeting woman, as I fondly thought of her, embodied the ephemeral nature of the performance I played many decades ago, where each moment is both transient and treasured. The fragility and transience of our roles for the time ahead.

Rising from my seat, drawn by an inexplicable force to search for something intangible yet deeply felt. It's as if the very walls around me whisper secrets and stories, urging me to uncover the soul of her within this place. And in this quest – the silent conversations, the unspoken understandings, and the shared moments that linger long after they've passed.

A poetic beauty in the way our lives intertwine, how our paths cross, and how we find each other in the vastness of existence. It's like a dance of souls, each step bringing us closer, each turn revealing a new facet of our being. Even the simplest gesture, meeting of lips, becomes a profound exchange, a silent conversation that speaks volumes. I am reminded of the importance of cherishing these connections and the places that hold them. They are the silent witnesses to our journey, the keepers of our stories, and the backdrop to the unfolding of our lives like a rose petal.

In her fleeting presence, captured the essence of transience that is so intrinsic to the art of performance. She runs down the Red Hallway to the ancient Greek gallery to find me...

In the performances of decades past, each moment on stage, a delicate dance between the transient and the treasured. The roles I embodied were fragile all those years ago, mirroring the fleeting nature of life itself...

These experiences, what we create are both momentary and meaningful. As the future unfolds, understanding this fragility and transience that shapes our approach to the art form we hold dear. The things we love and cherish. It's illuminated for all to see. A poetic beauty in the way our lives intertwine, how our paths cross, and how we find each other in the vastness of existence. It's like a dance of souls, each step bringing us closer, each turn revealing a new facet of our being. Even the simplest gesture, meeting of lips, becomes a profound exchange, a silent conversation that speaks volumes. I am reminded of the importance of cherishing these connections and the places that hold them. They are the silent witnesses to our journey, the keepers of our stories, and the backdrop to the unfolding of our lives like a rose petal.

The depths of human emotion and experience through our performances, creating art that resonates with the soul's ephemeral nature. The transient yet timeless art we will create. This world, our world, is for us to create. As I die again, I am reborn with you in this theatre with its drum beating within my chest. The crimson red fuel that you have laid within me. It has become all crystal clear to me, and I cannot wait to whisper it in your ear.

One last act before the night ends…

NEW YORK STATE OF MIND

I lay here on this bed, staring at the ceiling fan spinning around like the never-ending trauma that revolves in my head. The silence of this room is deafening. She left me a few weeks ago. Did I talk too much about the one event that protrudes at my weakest moments? Were my past experiences too much for her to bear? I will never know. The scent of her perfume still lingers in the air, a haunting reminder of her presence.

Outside, looters and rioters take to the streets. The distant sounds of shattering glass and shouts for help filter through the thin walls. I cannot even bear to turn on the television set without seeing my city burnt to the ground, and all for what? I will never know. Despite my anger at her leaving without any warning into the world of destruction, my instincts still yearn to know if she is okay. The taste of bitterness coats my tongue as I think of her.

Cannabis and cocaine have lost their sparkle. There is no use in breaking six years of sobriety from alcohol. That would be a torment to a slow death that I could not bear to take. People say I should just talk about it, but why? To stay misunderstood, to explain why I act the way I do when I am grieving? Why bother? Why talk about something that gives restless torment in my head without ceasing? The weight of my thoughts presses down on me, making it hard to breathe.

While swimming in this sea of anguish, my soul plunders into the bottomless pit where the demons await to devour the last of my innocence. I cling onto it as if it were the last possession to be torn from me. My personality is splitting into pieces while no relief is in sight, all the while my heart aches, parched. Burning me from within, my loathing turns finding my way out of this maze into a sheer impossibility. The cold sweat on my skin stays constant, reminding me of my insurmountable pain.

Acceptance is a cold, hard truth that I must live with. There is no running away from myself. Maybe she was right to run. How will I ever know? I suppose the love of God is still with me since I have not thought about taking my own life. However, I have had enough happy times in life. Learning to live with the scars, both seen and unseen, is the eternal curse while being alive. The taste of salt from my tears mixes with the feathers in my pillow.

Resigning to my suffering, I stay supine in the moonlight and plan any escape. The cool night air brushes against my skin, offering a fleeting moment of comfort. Maybe a New York state of mind could put rest on the soul.

I rush out of bed to flee my never-ending insomnia. With only the clothes on my back and wallet in my pocket, I dash to the nearest train station to flee from this city. In the crime-ridden streets of this post-industrial town, with smoke in the air, I hop on the train to fall into a slumber. By morning, I will wake up in the Big Apple. There is nothing left for me in this post-apocalyptic city where shells of automobile factories stand as stripped coffins of a bygone era.

Arriving at Grand Central Station, I open my bloodshot eyes with my back yearning to be stretched and unstiffened. I catch the next train to 110th Street and step off onto a dank subway station platform. This is what I came to do. Harlem.

As the sun sets over the city, casting a golden glow over the skyline, I take a deep breath and emerge from the subway platform. I step onto 110th Street. The city is a sensory overload. The smell of street food wafts through the air, mingling with the scent of exhaust fumes and cheap perfume. The never-ending wail of sirens tells my senses that the city is alive.

As I walk through Harlem, the vibrant culture is palpable. The rhythmic beats of jazz music spill out from open windows, blending with the laughter and conversations of people gathered on stoops and street corners. The murals and street art tell stories of resilience and hope, adding splashes of color to the brick buildings. The scent of soul food – fried chicken, collard greens, and cornbread – all remind me of the Eastside back home.

Neon signs flicker, casting colorful reflections on the wet sidewalks. I step into a nearby jazz club. I find a strange sense of solace in any jazz club I step into. I can let loose and be myself. No judgment. Swanky cats in their fine suits, taking a step off the street to have a good time.

95

I sit down at a small table and order a Shirley Temple. A lady takes notice of me nearby, staring at me as if she has an agenda. She walks over, offering me a cigarette, and that is when it happened. Flashback to that time of what haunts me. And so many.

White ash and burnt pieces of paper filled the air. A light grey covered everyone's faces. The sound of PASS Alarms going off in all directions. I didn't know where I was. From what I read in books; this is what they said a nuclear winter would look like. I see silhouettes staggering in the street. The Sun must be somewhere out there if I can see them, but if I can see them, where are the towers?

I snapped back into the present moment. The woman was sitting at the other end of my tiny table, saying, "It's not the lines off my body that is the issue. It's, why aren't we doing this right now?"

Fear ran down my spine. Was I talking and holding a conversation with a stranger this whole entire time? Out of all things I could have been talking about, that was what I uttered?

I ran out of the jazz club and jogged west as far as I could, as if I was running away from a bomb that I normally would love. I get to the Hudson River. Out of breath, I collapsed by the shore where I hyperventilated for a few minutes. Laying on the ground, my face was against the only patch of grass in sight. I stared at downtown. With its high towers and sparkling lights, I composed my breath but laid on the cool ground without hesitation. I felt relaxed as I always do when I looked at downtown.

As I lay there, the city lights twinkling like distant stars, I realized that running away wouldn't solve anything. The memories, the pain, the trauma – they were all a part of me. But so was the strength to get off of the ground. I took a deep breath, feeling the cool night air fill my lungs, and made a silent promise to myself. Finding peace in this chaotic world would no longer be a burden.

Reflections

Somewhere deep,
A soul begins to seep,
Beneath the soil, it creeps,
Up the roots of ancient trees,
To find life anew,
Wherever it may be.

G'night